FLORIDA

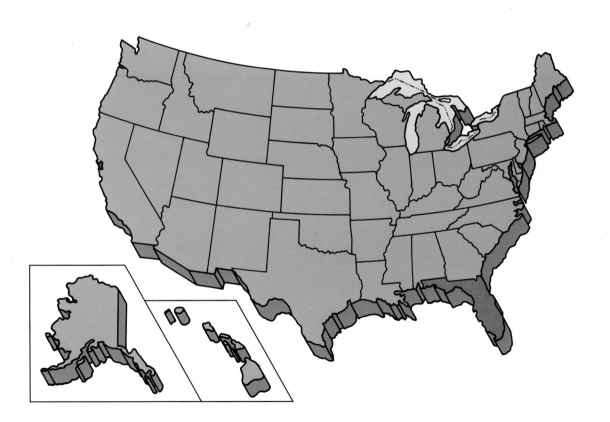

Hello U★S★A★

FLORIDA

Karen Sirvaitis

Lerner Publications Company

Cover photograph courtesy of Mike Kohn.

The glossary that begins on page 68 gives definitions of words shown in **bold type** in the text.

LIBRARY OF CONGRESS
CATALOGING-IN-PUBLICATION DATA
Sirvaitis, Karen.
    Florida / Karen Sirvaitis.
        p. cm. — (Hello USA)
    Includes index.
    Summary: Introduces the geography, history, environment, famous people, occupations, and culture of the Sunshine State.
        ISBN 0-8225-2728-6 (lib. bdg.)
    1. Florida—Juvenile literature.   2. Florida—Geography—Juvenile literature.   [1. Florida.]
    I. Title. II. Series.
    F311.3.S49   1994
    973—dc20   93-25402
                                                  CIP
                                                   AC

Manufactured in the United States of America

1 2 3 4 5 6 – I/JR – 99 98 97 96 95 94

 This book is printed on acid-free, recyclable paper.

CONTENTS

PAGE CHAPTER

6 Did You Know . . . ?
8 A Trip Around the State
19 Florida's Story
42 Living and Working in Florida
54 Protecting the Environment

SPECIAL SECTIONS

40 *Historical Timeline*
62 *Florida's Famous People*
66 *Facts-at-a-Glance*
68 *Pronunciation Guide, Glossary*
70 *Index*

Did You Know . . . ?

☐ The southernmost city of the mainland United States is Key West, Florida. It lies only 90 miles (145 kilometers) north of the island nation of Cuba.

☐ One of Florida's rivers has left its mark in music history. The Suwannee River was the subject of Stephen Foster's song "Old Folks at Home" (also known as "Swanee River"). The tune is now Florida's state song.

Key West is a popular winter vacation area.

❑ The rivers, lakes, and coastal waters of Florida host more varieties of fish than any other place in the world. Some colorful species include the cocoa damselfish and the queen angelfish.

❑ Florida is named in honor of *Pascua Florida,* an Easter festival held each year in Spain. Spanish explorer Juan Ponce de León gave Florida its name because he landed there the day of the celebration.

❑ Sanibel Island along the Gulf coast is called the Shelling Capital of the Western Hemisphere. The beaches of the island are sometimes layered knee-deep with billions of seashells.

A Trip Around the State

Beach balls, oranges, sunny days. These images of Florida match the state's nickname—the Sunshine State. Florida's many days of sunshine are such an attraction that some stores in the state sell cans that supposedly are filled with the warm, bright light.

Florida is a southern state. Georgia and Alabama are Florida's neighbors to the north, but most of Florida has borders that change with the tide. The powerful waves of the Atlantic Ocean wash against the state's eastern shore, while the Gulf of Mexico laps against the western shore. At the southern end of the state flows the Straits of Florida, a waterway that connects the Gulf and the ocean.

ALABAMA

GEORGIA

Perdido

OKEFENOKEE
SWAMP

St. Marys

TALLAHASSEE ☆

Jacksonville

Apalachicola

GULF
COASTAL PLAIN

Suwannee River

St. Augustine

St. Johns

FLORIDA
UPLANDS

ATLANTIC

OCEAN

Orlando

CAPE
CANAVERAL

ATLANTIC
COASTAL
PLAIN

GULF OF MEXICO

N

St. Petersburg

Tampa

GULF
COASTAL
PLAIN

*Lake
Okeechobee*

FLORIDA

Regional boundary

Miles
0   30   60
0   30   60
Kilometers

Sanibel
Island

*BIG
CYPRESS
SWAMP*

*THE
EVERGLADES*

Miami

EVERGLADES
NATIONAL
PARK

Florida Keys

Straits of Florida

Key West

Most of Florida is surrounded by water on three sides, forming a **peninsula**. The northernmost section of the state is called a panhandle because it is shaped somewhat like the handle of a frying pan. Florida's outline makes it one of the most noticeable states on a map, but Florida has not always been so easy to find. At one time, in fact, its land lay entirely under water.

Millions of years ago, Florida was an island. Volcanoes spewed out bubbling hot lava, threatening the island's plant life. The island was eventually buried by rising seawater, only to reappear as the level of the sea lowered. **Coral reefs,** or colorful underwater layers of limestone, began to form along the coast.

For thousands of years the sea level rose and fell, covering and then exposing Florida's coastline. The movement of the seawater helped form three land regions in the state—the Atlantic Coastal Plain, the Florida Uplands, and the Gulf Coastal Plain.

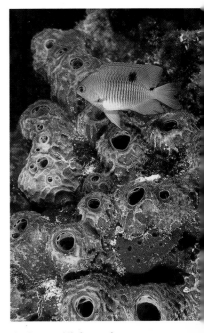

A damselfish cruises over sponges. These small sea animals have attached themselves to a coral reef. Many of Florida's small islands are made up of coral.

The Atlantic Coastal Plain, much of which is low and flat, stretches from north to south along eastern Florida. The region includes an offshore strip of islands and sandbars, or ridges of sand, that protect the coast from being thrashed by ocean waves. Shallow bodies of water called **lagoons** and grassy wetlands called **marshes** are sandwiched between the islands and the sparkling white coastal sands of the mainland.

The Florida Keys are situated at the southern tip of the Atlantic Coastal Plain. These islands curve

Thoroughbred horses are raised in the Florida Uplands region.

through the Straits of Florida into the Gulf of Mexico.

The Florida Uplands region runs across the northern half of the Panhandle and then cuts down into north central Florida, dividing the Gulf Coastal Plain into two parts. The northern uplands are hilly, and the southern portion of the region contains many shallow lakes.

The Gulf Coastal Plain covers almost all of western Florida. One section of this marshy region arcs across the southern portion of the Panhandle. The other half covers the southwestern part of the peninsula. Over the years, many of the area's marshes have been drained and filled with sand and soil to make the land solid enough to support homes and other structures.

Ten Thousand Islands, a group of many small islands in the Gulf of Mexico, are part of Everglades National Park.

But Florida is still home to some of the most famous wetlands in the nation. Big Cypress Swamp and The Everglades cover much of southern Florida. The Okefenokee Swamp straddles the border between Georgia and Florida.

13

Swamps are not the only inland bodies of water in Florida. The state's largest lake is Okeechobee, which covers nearly 700 square miles (1,813 sq km) of southern Florida. Lake Okeechobee, like most of Florida's lakes, is quite shallow. Its average depth is only about 8 feet (2.4 meters).

Florida's largest river is the Saint Johns. Other chief rivers include the Apalachicola, Perdido, and Saint Marys.

Breezes from the Atlantic Ocean and from the Gulf of Mexico cool Florida during the long, hot and humid summers. But even so, summer temperatures throughout the state average a steamy 83°F (28°C). During the winter, Floridians experience some relief

Fun on the Gulf of Mexico offers Floridians a break from the summer heat.

from the heat. Winter temperatures average 67°F (19°C) throughout the peninsula. Along the Panhandle, temperatures are slightly cooler.

Every summer and fall, tropical storms that produce severe winds, heavy rainfall, and high waves threaten Florida. Called hurricanes, these storms cause ocean waves to swell and flood coastal areas, sometimes bringing about many deaths and billions of dollars in damages.

Rainstorms are common in Florida. About 53 inches (135 centimeters) of rain fall each year in the state, some of it in the form of pounding thunderstorms. But the storm clouds quickly clear, permitting the Sunshine State to live up to its nickname.

The sun peeks out after a rain shower, creating a rainbow.

Orchid

A morning mist cloaks cypress trees in southern Florida.

Florida's generally warm and clear weather suits a variety of plants and animals. Mangroves— short trees whose jumbled-up roots crave salty ocean water— grow well along the coasts. Palm trees and forests of beech, bald cypress, magnolia, and pine cover about half the state. Beautiful tropical flowers, including orchids and lilies, grow wild in Florida.

Brown pelicans

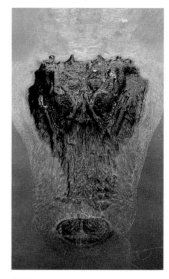

Alligator

Florida is home to large populations of waterbirds, including pelicans, herons, and flamingos. Black bears, deer, foxes, and wildcats roam Florida's forests. Bass, catfish, bluefish, marlins, red snappers, and sharks are common to the state's waters. Shellfish such as clams, crabs, crayfish, and oysters are found along the coasts. Alligators prowl through Florida's lakes, swamps, and rivers.

Florida's Story

The story of the first Floridians is a mystery. No one is certain when they arrived or where they came from. But many researchers believe that American Indians, or Native Americans, first reached the peninsula about 12,000 years ago. Some of them walked from the north. Others may have crossed the seas from the south.

Eventually, at least four major Native American nations, or tribes, made their homes in the area's forests and swamplands. The Calusa and the Tequesta lived in the south, and the Timucua and the Apalachee settled in the north. All four Indian groups used poles as frames for their homes. The branches of palmettos (palm trees with fan-shaped leaves) served as roofs.

A Timucua hunter disguises himself as a deer to fool his prey.

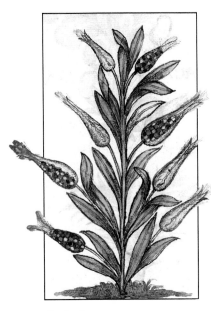

Early farmers grew maize, or corn, partly because it stayed fresh even when stored for the winter.

The groups in what is now Florida were skilled hunters and fishers. Using blowguns, bows and arrows, and clubs, hunters killed bears, wild turkeys, deer, and alligators to feed and clothe village members. Fishers speared their catch or trapped many fish at a time with underwater fences.

The Timucua and the Apalachee were good farmers as well, harvesting squash, corn, beans, and pumpkins. The Calusa and the Tequesta paddled dugout canoes southward to the Caribbean islands, where they traded goods with other tribes.

At least 100,000 American Indians lived in what is now Florida in 1513, when Spanish explorers landed their ship off the Atlantic coast near what is now Saint Augustine. Legend has it that the adventurers, led by Juan Ponce de León, were seeking the Fountain of Youth. The waters of this magical spring were rumored to restore health and youth to the sick and elderly.

The Timucua smoked their game over an open fire.

An artist pictured Ponce de León *(lower right)* searching high and low for the Fountain of Youth.

Whether the Spaniards actually searched for the fountain is not known for certain. Historians do know, however, that the Spaniards were looking for gold.

When Ponce de León did not find any gold, he left Florida. He returned in 1521, only to be wounded in a battle with the Calusa. The magical waters Ponce de León needed to cure himself were nowhere to be found, and the explorer died shortly afterward.

During the following 40 years, other Spanish explorers tried several times to set up a Spanish **colony,** or settlement, in Florida. All failed, conquered mainly by the wilderness, brutal weather, and fatal illness.

Alligators were only one of the many dangers lurking in the Florida wilderness.

F. Delfinum.

In 1564 Huguenots—a group of people who had left France to find religious freedom—built Fort Caroline, near present-day Jacksonville. From this site, the French were in a good position to attack and loot Spanish ships sailing from South America laden with gold and silver.

One year later, Spain sent Captain Pedro Menéndez de Avilés to drive the French out of Florida. Menéndez and his soldiers massacred most of the French settlers, who were caught unprotected at Fort Caroline. He then founded a Spanish settlement called Saint Augustine. The settlement firmly established Florida as a Spanish colony.

The Spaniards were very religious. They preached to the Indians, trying to persuade them to

24

Founded in 1565, Saint Augustine became the first permanent European settlement in what is now the United States.

give up their own religious beliefs and to become Catholics. Some Indians abandoned their lifelong religious beliefs, but most did not. Many were punished for refusing to convert.

From the mid-1500s to the mid-1700s, the Spaniards fought off many attackers, including the French and the British. Britain, which had established its own colonies along the Atlantic coast to the north of Florida, was one of Spain's oldest enemies and was eager for more land. During these attacks, hundreds of Indians living in Florida were captured and taken north to be sold as slaves in the British colonies.

In 1763 Spain gave Florida to Britain in exchange for Cuba, an island south of Florida. By this time, few Indians were living in the Florida colony. Most had either died from European diseases, had been sold into slavery, or had followed the Spaniards to Cuba.

At about the same time, thousands of Creek Indians, who had been forced from their homes in Georgia and Alabama by European settlers, moved southward into Florida. The Creek in Florida became known as the Seminoles.

The British divided Florida into two colonies. East Florida had its capital at Saint Augustine, and West Florida's capital became Pensacola. Most of the British settlers who came to the two colonies planted figs, sugarcane, cotton, indigo (a plant that yields a blue dye), and rice—crops suited to Florida's climate. Many of the planters used black slaves from Africa to work their **plantations,** or large farms.

In 1775 colonists in 13 of Britain's North American colonies began fighting the American War of Independence against Great Britain. The colonies no longer wanted to be ruled by a faraway king. They wanted instead to govern themselves.

The Floridas, however, stayed almost completely out of the revolution. Most Floridians had just recently left Britain for Florida, so

In the mid-1700s, British planters began growing rice in Florida. One planter brought about 1,200 people from Greece and Minorca (now a Spanish island) to farm his land. Many Floridians claim to be descendants of these workers.

they still felt loyal to the British king. In addition, the Floridas depended heavily on Britain for money.

But Britain's control over the Florida colonies was short-lived.

While British forces were busy fighting the war, Spain captured West Florida. In 1783 Britain lost the revolution and decided to return East Florida to Spain. Meanwhile, the 13 colonies united and formed one country—the United States of America. Florida would soon fly the same flag.

Spanish settlers again moved into the Floridas and so did Americans. Some Americans took over abandoned British plantations. Others built homes on Seminole land. By the early 1800s, Americans outnumbered Spaniards in the Floridas.

In 1821 the U.S. flag replaced the Spanish flag in Florida. General Andrew Jackson *(inset)* briefly served as governor of the new territory.

Osceola (1803?–1838) organized the Seminoles to fight for their land during the Second Seminole War. After waging many successful attacks against several U.S. generals, Osceola was captured late in 1837. He died shortly afterward in prison.

Angry that so many Americans were taking Indian land, the Seminoles attacked the settlers. In 1817 General Andrew Jackson led U.S. soldiers into battle against the Seminole Indians. The First Seminole War ended in 1818 with a victory for Jackson. More wars would follow.

The U.S. military intervention left Spain feeling powerless in the Floridas. In 1821 Spain decided to give the colonies to the United States for $5 million. Three years later, the United States merged East and West Florida into one territory and chose Tallahassee as the capital city.

Once again, Americans poured into Florida. Many were farmers interested in the fertile lands of northern Florida—Seminole territory. In 1835 fights over who owned this land helped start the Second Seminole War—the most expensive Indian conflict in U.S. history.

The Seminole Freedmen

The First and Second Seminole wars were fought over more than just land. They were also fought over the freedom of escaped slaves who came to be known as the Seminole Freedmen, or the Seminole blacks.

During and after the War of Independence, black slaves from Georgia and the Carolinas fled to Spanish Florida, where the Seminole Indians welcomed the runaways. Many of these blacks were tasting freedom for the first time. Because they spoke English better than most Seminoles, some Freedmen became tribal leaders and influenced decisions made by the Seminole nation.

In the early 1800s, plantation owners complained to the U.S. government that the Seminoles harbored escaped slaves. The U.S. Army tried to capture and return the runaways. The Seminoles chose to fight for the Freedmen, who were an important part of the Seminole nation. This decision sparked both Seminole wars.

Costing the United States at least $20 million and 1,500 lives, the conflict lasted seven years. The Seminoles also paid a heavy price. Some Seminoles fled to The Everglades, but most either died from disease or wounds or were moved far away to Oklahoma.

With most of the Indians gone, even more Americans came to Florida to grow cotton on the Panhandle and sugarcane on the peninsula. The planters brought thousands of slaves to Florida. Of the more than 45,000 people in the territory in the 1840s, half of them were black slaves.

In the middle of Florida's flag is the state seal. It pictures rays of sunshine and a palm tree for Florida's warm climate, a steamboat to represent transportation, and a Native American woman scattering flowers.

In 1845 Florida had enough white residents to become a state. On March 3, 1845, Florida became the 27th state of the Union. But by this time, the country was on the verge of breaking up. Northern and Southern states disagreed over many issues, including slavery.

31

Stooping over all day to pick cotton was hard work.

Northerners, many of whom worked in factories, had outlawed slavery in their states. Southerners, however, still made a living largely from the growing and selling of crops. To be properly maintained, plantations required a large workforce. Southern planters argued that without slave labor, they could not afford to run the farms and still make a profit.

In 1861 Florida and other Southern states formed the Confederate States of America (the Confederacy), a nation where slavery would be legal. Shortly afterward, Southern forces attacked a Union fort in the Confederate state of South Carolina, and the Civil War began.

Union troops immediately captured Florida's coastal cities, but few battles were fought in the state. Florida's major role in the Civil War was to supply beef, pork, salt, and sugar to Confederate troops.

The Confederacy lost the war in 1865. Austin, in Texas, and Tallahassee were the only two Confederate state capitals that had not been occupied by Union troops. After the war, the Union made its presence known in Tallahassee and elsewhere in the South.

A period of reform called **Reconstruction** brought Northern troops, politicians, and teachers into the South to make changes. The 70,000 slaves in Florida had been freed.

Schools were built for the African American children, and African American men were given the right to vote and to hold public office.

In 1875 eight African Americans were members of Florida's House of Representatives. Three are pictured above on the steps of the state capitol.

In the late 1800s, two-fifths of Florida was soggy wetland, unsuitable for growing crops and building homes. So the state both sold its land at low prices and gave it away to anyone willing to drain the swamps and marshes and build something that would encourage people to move to the state.

Florida's government gave most of the free land to railroad companies. By train, people and goods could easily reach remote areas. And farmers could now ship their

Workers crate oranges at a citrus plant in Florida.

citrus fruits to northern markets, where the climate was too cold for growing grapefruits and oranges.

The trains also brought tourists. Florida's warm winter climate and beautiful coastline made the state an attractive resort area for vacationers. Dozens of hotels sprang up, creating the resort towns of Miami Beach, Coral Gables, Key West, Palm Beach, Tampa, Clearwater, and Saint Petersburg. Land sales in Florida skyrocketed as people realized they could make millions of dollars selling beachfront property.

Elegant hotels, such as this one in Green Cove Springs, Florida, were built in the late 1800s.

FLORIDA'S MOST FAMOUS HENRIES

During the late 1800s, at least two business leaders took advantage of the land given away by Florida's state government. Henry M. Flagler (1830–1913) and Henry B. Plant (1819–1899) built up Florida's coasts, boosting the state's economy and helping turn Florida into a major tourist attraction.

Flagler concentrated on Florida's east coast. One of his major accomplishments was to help organize the Florida East Coast Railway, which by 1912 had stretched from Jacksonville all the way to Key West. Flagler also built hotels in Saint Augustine, Palm Beach, Miami, and other seaside cities.

Plant worked on Florida's west coast. He purchased a string of railroads that eventually connected Florida with the northern United States. In 1886 Plant bought a fleet of steamships to carry goods to and from Florida and the Caribbean islands. Plant also built hotels, including the lavish Tampa Bay Hotel.

By the 1890s, Florida was booming. Miners had discovered that central Florida covered large deposits of phosphate rock, a mineral used to make fertilizers. A tobacco processor named Vicente Martinez Ybor established a thriving cigar industry in Tampa. Cattle, which had originally been brought to Florida by Juan Ponce de León, were being raised on a large scale in central Florida.

Workers at a cigar factory in Tampa handpick leaves for wrapping individual cigars.

In 1898 the United States became involved in a revolution taking place in Cuba, which was still ruled by Spain. Most Cubans wanted to be free of Spanish rule, and the U.S. government sided with the Cubans. During the Span-ish-American War, military bases were built on Florida's coast. The state expanded its military role during World War I (1914–1918), when it became a major ship-building center.

Two deadly hurricanes, one in 1926 and another in 1928, put an end to Florida's boom. More than 2,000 people were killed in the hurricanes that struck southern Florida by surprise.

The state saw more hard times with the beginning of the Great Depression in 1929. This slump in the nation's economy lasted about 10 years. Banks closed, railroad companies lost money, and tourism declined.

U.S. Navy pilots practice flying bomber planes over Miami during World War II.

In the 1950s, motels began to advertise that their rooms were air conditioned.

The nation's economy turned around during World War II (1939–1945). Florida became the site of more U.S. military bases. The state's usually clear skies allowed air force pilots to practice takeoffs and landings almost daily. Florida's glitzy hotels were temporarily turned into hospitals and training camps.

After the United States and its allies won the war, many of Florida's military bases remained active. In 1950 the U.S. government established Cape Canaveral, a missile-testing site on Florida's

Atlantic coast. In 1963 the National Aeronautics and Space Administration (NASA) opened the John F. Kennedy Space Center near Cape Canaveral. NASA's first goal was to put a person on the moon. The space center accomplished this mission in 1969.

The 1960s saw a great increase in Florida's population. As air conditioning became common, more people could tolerate Florida's hot summers, and elderly people from northern states moved to Florida to escape from the cold winters.

Thousands of other newcomers sailed from Cuba and Haiti, two island countries located just south of Florida. The **immigrants** hoped to find better jobs, better homes, and more freedom than they had experienced in their homelands.

In 1986 part of the space program at Cape Canaveral came to a halt. In January of that year, the space shuttle *Challenger* exploded just after take-off, killing all seven crew members. The accident marked the greatest tragedy in NASA's history.

The *Apollo 11* spacecraft and its crew members were the first to land on the moon.

| 10,000 B.C. | A.D.1513 | 1565 | 1763 | 1783 | 1821 | 1835 | 1845 |

Native Americans first arrive in what is now Florida

Juan Ponce de León searches for the Fountain of Youth

Pedro Menéndez de Avilés founds Saint Augustine

Spain gives Florida to Britain

Spain regains control of Florida

Spain gives Florida to the United States

Second Seminole War (1835–1842) begins

Florida becomes the 27th state

Another disaster occurred in Florida in August of 1992. Hurricane Andrew struck the Atlantic and Gulf coasts with howling winds blowing 160 miles (257 km) per hour. Andrew killed dozens of people, destroyed billions of dollars worth of property, and left thousands of Floridians homeless and without food or water.

Tent and trailer colonies were set up to provide homes, food, and

40

1861	1895	1950	1969	1992
★	★	★	★	★

Floridians supply foodstuffs to Confederate soldiers during the Civil War (1861–1865)

Henry Flagler establishes the Florida East Coast Railway

Cape Canaveral opens

Apollo 11 is launched from Cape Canaveral

Hurricane Andrew

The remains of a trailer park in Homestead, Florida, show the destruction caused by Hurricane Andrew.

clothing for those people who lost their property in the hurricane. Rebuilding the areas damaged by Hurricane Andrew has taken a lot of work, but most Floridians once again have a place they call home.

Living and Working in Florida

Chances are good that if you meet a Floridian on the street, you'll discover that he or she was not born in Florida. The Sunshine State attracts people from all over the world, and newcomers have made Florida one of the fastest growing states in the nation.

The state's population rose above 13 million in 1990, an increase of 33 percent since 1980. Most Floridians live in one of the state's five largest cities—Jacksonville, Miami, Tampa, and Saint Petersburg. Tallahassee has been Florida's capital city since 1824.

Downtown Miami

42

A band member in Bradenton, Florida, plays the clarinet.

Although most Floridians were born in the United States, about one out of ten people in the state moved from other countries, including Great Britain, Germany, Canada, Cuba, and Puerto Rico.

Newspapers and signs printed in Spanish are found throughout Miami. Many Cubans (who speak Spanish) settled in this city after making life-threatening journeys on small and overcrowded boats to escape difficulties in their homeland. Florida's **Latinos**, most of whom are of Cuban descent, make up 12 percent of the state's population.

Blacks make up 14 percent of Florida's population. Most Native Americans were removed to Oklahoma after the Second Seminole War, but small numbers of Seminoles still remain in Florida.

Mickey Mouse and his pals are such well-known residents of Florida that they might as well be included in the state's population figures. The world's most famous mouse came to Florida when Walt Disney World Resort opened near Orlando in 1971. Since then, Mickey Mouse, Minnie Mouse, Goofy, Donald Duck, and Pluto have entertained thousands of vacationers every year. But visiting the animated characters at Walt Disney World is only the beginning of what people can see and do in Florida.

Magic Kingdom, a theme park that attracts millions of visitors each year, is part of Walt Disney World Resort.

Macaws pose at the Parrot Jungle and Gardens, located just south of Miami.

A scene from *Indiana Jones and the Last Crusade* is made lifelike at Disney-MGM Studios in Orlando.

Busch Gardens in Tampa is an adventure for all. A stroll through the zoo leads you past African lions and tigers. The amusement park in the gardens offers dozens of thrilling rides. At Parrot Jungle and Gardens in Miami, parrots and monkeys perform all kinds of tricks. Near Orlando, Sea World of Florida is a splash when Shamu, the "Killer Whale," performs for audiences.

John Pennekamp Coral Reef State Park off the island of Key Largo was the first underwater park established in the mainland

46

United States. Those who aren't afraid of what might lurk in the sea can go diving to examine the reefs up close. Others can view the colorful formations from a glass-bottom boat.

In eastern Florida, along what is known as the Space Coast, people can imagine what it would be like to be an astronaut by visiting the John F. Kennedy Space Center. Just south of the Space Coast lies the Treasure Coast, where divers still find precious booty from Spanish ships that sank in the 1500s.

These are only a few of the hundreds of attractions in Florida. One of the state's most popular events is the Orange Bowl, a college football game played every New Year's

A *Discovery* space shuttle prepares to launch from the John F. Kennedy Space Center.

Day in Miami. The Gator Bowl in Jacksonville and the Florida Citrus Bowl in Orlando are other college football events held each year in the state.

A Los Angeles Dodger signs autographs during spring training in Florida.

Professional sports teams in Florida include football's Miami Dolphins, soccer's Tampa Bay Rowdies, and basketball's Miami Heat. Baseballs fly through the air every spring, when 18 major-league teams from cold, northern states come to Florida to warm up for the baseball season.

When they aren't having fun in the sun, Floridians work in a variety of jobs. About 80 percent of Florida's workers have service jobs—that is, they help other people and businesses. Service workers in Florida include the lifeguards

Service workers prepare salads in a restaurant kitchen in Florida.

who watch over swimmers and the hotel desk clerks who give vacationers the keys to beachfront rooms. The agents who buy and sell resorts and retirement homes and the salesclerks who sell cans of sunshine to tourists are also service workers.

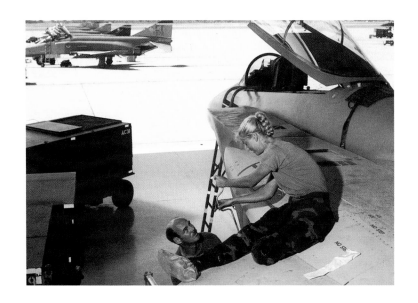

U.S. Air Force pilots work on a military plane at Eglin Air Force Base in Fort Walton Beach, Florida.

Some service workers have jobs with the government. They include the governor, national and state park workers, and employees at the John F. Kennedy Space Center. Several military bases closed in the early 1990s, costing the state about 12,000 service jobs, but thousands of soldiers are still trained and stationed at the remaining bases in the state.

Florida is also a leading manufacturing state. Companies in the state produce equipment needed to

run the space programs at Cape Canaveral. To make fertilizer, Florida continues to mine its large supply of phosphate rock. Many Floridians squeeze grapefruits, oranges, and lemons into juices. Oranges are also boiled to make marmalade.

Citrus farmers in south central Florida grow most of the nation's oranges—about two-thirds—along with tons of grapefruits, limes, tangerines, and lemons. Other fruits come from the state's banana trees and strawberry patches.

51

Radishes *(facing page, top)*
Cattle *(facing page, bottom)*
Shrimp boats *(left)*

Florida produces more sugarcane and more houseplants than any other state. Tomatoes and cotton are other chief crops. Livestock farmers raise mostly beef and dairy cattle.

The fishing industry in Florida makes millions of dollars catching fish and shellfish from the state's coastal waters. Shrimp, lobsters, and scallops bring in the most money. Popular saltwater fish include grouper, mackerel, and red snapper. Catfish is the leading freshwater catch.

A large portion of Florida's fish, shellfish, citrus fruits, and other goods are shipped to other states. Tampa, along the Gulf coast, is the state's leading port, handling about 50 million tons (45 million metric tons) of incoming and outgoing goods a year.

Florida's clear, warm waters provide ideal growing conditions for coral reefs.

Protecting the Environment

Florida is the only place in North America with a long line of coral reefs in its shallow coastal waters. Thousands of colorful reefs are located along the state's coast. In some places, the seawater is so clear and shallow that the beautiful patterns and colors of the reefs can be viewed from ashore.

Coral reefs flourish along Florida's coast because the waters are warm and clear. Every year, these reefs attract thousands of visitors wanting to explore the delicate underwater coral gardens. But some of these people are careless, accidentally destroying some of Florida's reefs each year.

Divers are warned to be gentle while exploring Florida's coral reefs.

This huge brain coral is made up of layers and layers of coral polyps.

Coral reefs are made up of both living and nonliving elements. The foundation of a coral reef is limestone. The limestone is actually produced by colonies of tiny sea animals called **coral polyps,** which secrete a coating of limestone around part of their bodies. When the colonies die, these limestone skeletons contribute to a reef's growth. Because polyps are so small, reefs grow slowly—only 1 to 16 feet (30 to 490 cm) every 1,000 years!

Coral reefs serve many purposes. They provide shelter, food, and breeding sites for many underwater plants and animals. They also break strong waves, naturally protecting Florida's coasts.

Coral reefs shelter a rich variety of plant and animal life, including feather-duster worms.

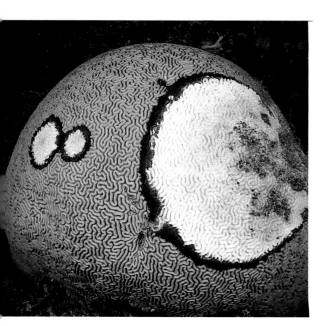

The infection on this brain coral could destroy all its living coral colonies.

As solid as they may seem, coral reefs are actually very fragile. By simply standing on or scraping a coral colony, for instance, divers can start a chain reaction. Broken or scraped coral might become infected and die. The infection could spread and kill an entire colony. Boaters and fishers also start these infections by grounding their boats on coral reefs, hitting the reefs with anchors, or scraping them with fishing spears.

In addition, coral reefs, which need clear, clean water to grow, die quickly when exposed to pollution. Because water pollution comes from so many sources, in-

Farmers fertilize their crops to help them grow. But rainwater washes excess fertilizer into the ocean, polluting the water and endangering coral reefs.

cluding septic tanks and farms, it is one of the most difficult problems to attack.

To help protect areas of coral, the state of Florida opened the John Pennekamp Coral Reef State Park—the world's first underwater marine park—in the 1960s. In the 1970s, the U.S. government created what has now become the Florida Keys National Marine Sanctuary—another area of protected coral reefs. Removing coral, anchoring or grounding boats on coral, throwing garbage into the water, using spear guns or wire fish traps, and even standing on coral are all against the law in the sanctuary.

59

Careful boaters can still enjoy Florida's coral reefs.

Despite everything you can't do in the sanctuary, the government does make it possible for visitors to enjoy the reefs. People can still boat, swim, and dive in the sanctuary as long as they are careful. But the sanctuary may limit fishing, jet skiing, diving, treasure hunting, boating, and docking in areas most likely to be damaged from these activities.

In the sanctuary, a warning not to stand on or around coral is distributed in English, Spanish, German, Japanese, French, and Italian. It's a simple message, reminding Floridians and tourists from around the world that in a matter of seconds they can destroy what took nature thousands of years to create.

Florida's Famous People

◀ ASA PHILIP RANDOLPH

ACTIVISTS ■■■■■■■■■■■■■■■■■■■■■■■■■

John D. Pennekamp (1897–1978) helped establish Everglades National Park and John Pennekamp Coral Reef State Park. An editor of the *Miami Herald*, Pennekamp lived in Miami for more than 50 years.

Asa Philip Randolph (1889–1979), born in Crescent City, Florida, worked to gain rights for laborers. Randolph persuaded Presidents Roosevelt and Truman to give African Americans a fair chance at government jobs. In 1957 Randolph became a vice president of a powerful labor union called the AFL-CIO.

JOHN PENNEKAMP ▶

▼ SIDNEY POITIER

ACTORS ■■■■■■■■■■■■■■■■■■■■■■

Faye Dunaway (born 1941), an actress from Bascom, Florida, first made it big as gangster Bonnie Parker in the 1967 film *Bonnie and Clyde*. She has played leading roles in many other movies, including *Chinatown*, *Three Days of the Condor*, and *Mommie Dearest*. Dunaway received an Academy Award for her performance in *Network*.

Sidney Poitier (born 1927), from Miami, has starred in several films that address racial problems in the United States. His film credits include *The Blackboard Jungle* and *Guess Who's Coming to Dinner*. In 1963 Poitier won an Academy Award for his performance in *Lilies of the Field*.

Burt Reynolds (born 1936) spent much of his childhood in West Palm Beach, Florida. After a knee injury ruined his chances

▲ FAYE DUNAWAY

BURT REYNOLDS ▶

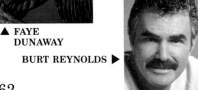

in professional football, Reynolds turned to acting. His performance in the 1972 motion picture *Deliverance* made him famous, launching him into starring roles in *Smokey and the Bandit* and a popular television show called "Evening Shade."

ATHLETES

Anthony Carter (born 1960), from Miami, is a wide receiver for the Minnesota Vikings. While playing college football for the University of Michigan, Carter was named to the All-American team three years in a row. He has played in the Pro Bowl twice.

Chris Evert (born 1954) is a world champion tennis player who grew up in Fort Lauderdale, Florida. The daughter of a tennis instructor, Evert began playing the game at age six. Evert, who retired from tournament competition in 1989, won more titles (157) and matches (1,300) than any of her contemporaries.

ANTHONY
▼ CARTER

▲ CHRIS EVERT

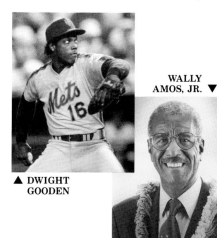

WALLY
AMOS, JR. ▼

▲ DWIGHT
GOODEN

Dwight ("Dr. K") Gooden (born 1964), a pitcher, joined the New York Mets in 1984 at the age of 19. In 1985 Gooden became the youngest athlete ever to win the National League's Cy Young Award, the highest honor for pitchers. His fastballs, traveling as fast as 96 miles (154 km) per hour, have struck out many batters. Gooden is originally from Tampa.

BUSINESS LEADERS

Wallace ("Wally") Amos, Jr. (born 1936), founded the Famous Amos Chocolate Chip Cookie Company in Los Angeles, California, in 1975. Wally's cookies became wildly popular after people learned that many Hollywood stars loved the taste. Amos was born in Tallahassee.

Vicente Martinez Ybor (1818–1896), a native of Spain, built Tampa's first cigar factory in the 1880s, starting the city's cigar-making industry. Ybor City, now a Cuban neighborhood in Tampa, was once a settlement for Martinez's factory workers.

Charles Edward Merrill (1885–1956) from Green Cove Springs, Florida, began a small investment business in 1914. By 1941 it grew to become Merrill, Lynch, Pierce, Fenner & Beane (now Merrill Lynch & Co.)—the largest brokerage firm in the world at the time.

◀ VICENTE MARTINEZ YBOR

CHARLES MERRILL ▶

MUSICIANS

GLORIA ESTEFAN ▶

▼ MEL TILLIS

▲ JIM MORRISON

Gloria Estefan (born 1957), a Cuban American songwriter and singer, grew up in Miami. Estefan is the lead singer for the Miami Sound Machine (MSM), a band that performs ballads and dance music with a Latin beat. The group's hit songs include "Conga" and "Get on Your Feet."

Jim Morrison (1943–1971), a singer and songwriter, formed a rock band called the Doors in 1965 with organist Ray Manzarek. The group's best-selling albums include *Waiting for the Sun* and *L.A. Woman.* Morrison was born in Melbourne, Florida.

Tom Petty (born 1952) is a singer, songwriter, and guitar player from Gainesville, Florida. In 1975 he formed the rock group Tom Petty and the Heartbreakers. The band's best-known hits include "Refugee" and "Don't Do Me Like That."

Mel Tillis (born 1932), a country singer and songwriter from Pahokee, Florida, has written more than 450 songs, including "Ruby Don't Take Your Love to Town."

Janet Reno (born 1938), from Miami, served as Florida's state attorney for 15 years, starting in 1978. In 1993 she became the first woman to be appointed U.S. attorney general, the nation's "top cop."

Xavier Suarez (born 1949), the first Cuban American mayor of Miami, served from 1985 to 1993. Suarez led the city through many difficulties, including riots and drug wars.

▼ JANET RENO

▲ XAVIER SUAREZ

ZORA NEALE ▶
HURSTON

▲ ERNEST HEMINGWAY

JAMES WELDON ▶
JOHNSON

WRITERS

Ernest Hemingway (1899–1961) is remembered for his simple and honest writing style. Many of Hemingway's novels are based on his experiences in different locations, including the Florida Keys. While in Florida, Hemingway worked on *To Have and Have Not, A Farewell to Arms,* and *For Whom the Bell Tolls*—three of his most famous novels.

Zora Neale Hurston (1903–1960), born in Eatonville, Florida, wrote *Mules and Men,* a collection of folktales about southern blacks living in rural communities. Her most famous novel is *Their Eyes Were Watching God.*

James Weldon Johnson (1871–1938), born in Jacksonville, wrote a well-known novel about racism entitled *The Autobiography of an Ex-Colored Man.* He also wrote the lyrics to the song "Lift Ev'ry Voice and Sing," which is considered a national anthem by many African Americans. In 1993 the song was published as an illustrated children's book.

Facts-at-a-Glance ━━━━━━━

Nickname: Sunshine State
Song: "Old Folks at Home"
Motto: In God We Trust
Flower: orange blossom
Tree: sabal palm
Bird: mockingbird

Population: 12,937,926*
Rank in population, nationwide: 4th
Area: 65,758 sq mi (170,313 sq km)
Rank in area, nationwide: 22nd
Date and ranking of statehood:
  March 3, 1845, the 27th state
Capital: Tallahassee (124,773*)
Major cities (and populations*):
  Jacksonville (672,971), Miami (358,548),
  Tampa (280,015), Saint Petersburg (238,629)
U.S. senators: 2
U.S. representatives: 23
Electoral votes: 25

Places to visit: Everglades Wonder Gardens in Bonita Springs, Miccosukee Indian Village near Miami, Ringling Museum of Art in Sarasota, Spaceport USA on Merritt Island, Museum of Discovery and Science in Fort Lauderdale, Walt Disney World Resort in Lake Buena Vista

Annual events: Zora Neale Hurston Festival of Arts in Eatonville (Jan.), Silver Spurs Rodeo in Kissimmee (Feb.), Annual Sanibel Shell Fair (March), Flying High Circus in Tallahassee (March), Aquafest in Melbourne (June), Maritime Festival in Saint Augustine (Oct.)

*1990 census

Natural resources: limestone, phosphate rock, forests, sandy beaches

Agricultural products: oranges, grapefruits, limes, lemons, strawberries, bananas, tomatoes, cabbage, sugarcane, houseplants, beef cattle, milk

Manufactured goods: communication equipment, X-ray equipment, citrus fruit juices, canned sections of fruit, newspapers, books, aerospace and aircraft equipment, computers, fertilizer

ENDANGERED SPECIES
Mammals—finback whale, Florida panther, gray bat, Key deer, Lower Keys marsh rabbit, West Indian manatee
Birds—Cape Sable seaside sparrow, ivory-billed woodpecker, Kirtland's warbler, wood stork
Corals—pillar coral
Reptiles—American crocodile, Atlantic green turtle
Fish—shortnose sturgeon, Okaloosa darter
Plants—wild columbine, dwarf spleenwart, Florida bonamia

WHERE FLORIDIANS WORK
Services—66 percent
   (services includes jobs in trade; community, social, & personal services; finance, insurance, & real estate; transportation, communication, & utilities)
Government—15 percent
Manufacturing—10 percent
Construction—6 percent
Agriculture—3 percent

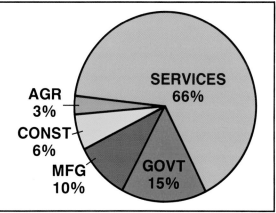

AGR 3%
CONST 6%
MFG 10%
SERVICES 66%
GOVT 15%

Apalachee (ap-uh-LACH-ee)

Apalachicola (ap-uh-lach-uh-KOH-luh)

Calusa (kuh-LOO-suh)

Cape Canaveral (kayp kuh-NAV-ruhl)

Haiti (HAYT-ee)

Huguenot (HYOO-guh-naht)

Menéndez de Avilés, Pedro
(may-NAYN-dayth day ah-vee-LAYS,
PAY-droh)

Okeechobee (oh-kuh-CHOH-bee)

Okefenokee (oh-kuh-fuh-NOH-kee)

Seminole (SEHM-uh-nohl)

Tallahassee (tal-uh-HAS-ee)

Tequesta (tee-KWEHS-tuh)

Timucua (tihm-uh-KOO-uh)

Glossary

colony A territory ruled by a country some distance away.

coral polyp A small, tube-shaped sea animal. The limestone skeletons of coral polyps form the hard base of coral reefs.

coral reef A ridge of rocklike formations made up of billions of coral polyp skeletons. Coral reefs are found in warm, shallow seas.

immigrant A person who moves into a foreign country and settles there.

lagoon A shallow lake or pond, especially one that joins a larger body of water.

Latino A person living in the United States who either came from or has ancestors from Latin America. Latin America includes Mexico and most of Central and South America.

marsh A spongy wetland soaked with water for long periods of time. Marshes are usually treeless; grasses are the main form of vegetation found in marshes.

peninsula A stretch of land almost completely surrounded by water.

plantation A large estate, usually in a warm climate, on which crops are grown by workers who live on the estate. In the past, plantation owners usually used slave labor.

Reconstruction The period from 1865 to 1877 during which the U.S. government brought the Southern states back into the Union after the Civil War. Before rejoining the Union, a Southern state had to pass a law allowing black men to vote. Places destroyed in the war were rebuilt and industries were developed.

Index

African Americans, 26, 30, 32, 33, 44. *See also* Seminole Freedmen

Agriculture, 20, 26, 27, 29, 30, 32, 33, 34–35, 37, 51–53, 59. *See also* Cattle; Citrus fruits; Cotton; Sugarcane

Air conditioning, 38, 39

Alabama, 8, 26

Alligators, 17, 20, 23

Animals, 12, 16–17, 20, 46. *See also* Alligators

Atlantic Coastal Plain, 11–13

Atlantic Ocean, 8, 14, 15, 40, 59

Beaches, 7, 8, 12, 14

Britain, 25–27, 28, 44

Cape Canaveral, 38–39, 51

Caribbean islands, 20, 36, 39, 44. *See also* Cuba

Cattle, 33, 37, 52, 53

Cities and towns, 24, 26, 33, 35, 41, 44, 50. *See also* Cape Canaveral; Jacksonville; Key West; Miami; Orlando; Saint Augustine; Saint Petersburg; Tallahassee; Tampa

Citrus fruits, 8, 34–35, 51, 53

Climate, 8, 14–16, 23, 26, 31, 35, 37, 39, 40–41, 57

Coastline, 7, 8, 11, 15, 16, 20, 35, 39, 40, 47, 54, 57

Confederate States of America (the Confederacy), 32–33

Coral reefs, 11, 46–47, 54–61

Cotton, 26, 30, 32, 53

Cuba, 6, 26, 37, 39, 44

East Florida, 26, 27, 29

Economy, 34, 35, 36, 37, 38, 39, 40–41, 48–53

Environment, 54–61

Ethnic makeup, 24, 28, 29, 30–31, 39, 44

European countries, 20, 24, 25–27, 44. *See also* Britain; Spain

Everglades, The, 13, 30

Fish, sea life, and fishing, 7, 11, 17, 20, 46–47, 52–53, 56–61. *See also* Coral reefs

Flag, 31

Flagler, Henry M., 36

Florida: boundaries and location, 6, 8, 11; ethnic makeup, 24, 28, 29, 30–31, 39, 44; Facts-at-a-Glance, 66–67; Famous People, 62–65; flag of, 31; maps and charts, 10; nicknames, 8, 15, 42; origin of name, 7; population, 39, 42; statehood, 31

Florida Keys, 12–13, 46. *See also* Key West

Florida Panhandle, 11, 13, 15, 30

Florida peninsula, 11, 15, 19, 20, 30

Florida Uplands, 11, 12, 13

Forests, 16, 17, 19

Foster, Stephen, 6

Georgia, 8, 13, 26

Gold, 23, 24
Gulf Coastal Plain, 11, 13
Gulf of Mexico, 7, 8, 13, 14,
  40, 53

Health, 20, 23, 26, 30
History, 18-41; ancient, 11,
  19-20; colonial, 25-27; 1800s,
  28-37; exploration and trade,
  7, 20, 22-23; 1500s-1700s,
  20-27; independence, 26-27;
  1900s, 37-41; settlers, 24-26,
  28-30; statehood, 31; timeline,
  40-41
Hurricanes, 15, 37, 40-41

Indians, 18-20, 24-26, 29-30,
  31, 44; Apalachee, 19, 20;
  Calusa, 19, 20, 23; Creek, 26;
  Seminoles, 26, 28-30, 44; Tequesta, 19, 20; Timucua,
  18-19, 20, 21
Islands, 7, 11, 12, 13

Jackson, Andrew, 28, 29
Jacksonville, 24, 42, 47
Jobs, 32, 34, 39, 48-51, 53
John F. Kennedy Space Center,
  39, 47, 50
John Pennekamp Coral Reef
  State Park, 46, 59

Key West, 6, 35, 36

Lakes, 7, 13, 14, 17

Manufacturing and industries,
  34, 37, 50-51
Martinez Ybor, Vincente, 37
Menéndez de Avilés, Pedro, 24
Miami, 38, 42-43, 46, 47, 48
Military, 24, 29, 32-33, 37, 38,
  50
Mining and minerals, 23, 24,
  37, 51

National Aeronautics and Space
  Adminstration (NASA), 39,
  47, 51. *See also* John F.
  Kennedy Space Center
Native Americans. *See* Indians

Orlando, 45, 46, 47
Osceola, 29

Plant, Henry B., 36
Plants, 16, 57
Pollution, 54-61
Ponce de León, Juan, 7, 20,
  22-23, 37
Population, 39, 42

Railroads, 34-35, 36, 37

Religion, 24-25
Rivers, 6, 7, 14, 17

Saint Augustine, 20, 24, 25,
  26, 36
Saint Petersburg, 35, 42
Seminole Freedmen, 30
Slavery, 25, 26, 30, 31-32, 33, 44
Spain, 7, 20, 22-23, 24-25, 26,
  27, 28, 29, 37
Sports and recreation, 45-48,
  54-55, 58, 59, 60
Straits of Florida, 8, 13
Sugarcane, 26, 27, 30, 33, 53

Tallahassee, 29, 33, 42
Tampa, 35, 37, 42, 46, 48, 53
Tourism, 6, 35, 36, 37, 45-47,
  49, 54, 60
Transportation, 20, 24, 34-35,
  36, 37, 53

United States of America, 27,
  29-30, 37-38

Walt Disney World Resort, 45
Wars and battles, 23, 24, 25,
  26-27, 29-30, 32-33, 37, 38, 44
West Florida, 26, 27, 29
Wetlands, 12, 13, 14, 34

Acknowledgments:

Maryland Cartographics, pp. 2, 10; Donna L. Hupp / Laatsch-Hupp Photo, pp. 2-3; Rick Poley, pp. 6, 15, 48; Jack Lindstrom, p. 7; Frederica Georgia, pp. 8-9, 12, 17 (left), 46 (left); © Adam Jones, pp. 11, 16 (left), 55, 56; NE Stock Photos: © Clyde H. Smith, p. 13, © Peter Randall, p. 23, © Frank Siteman, pp. 41, 42-43, © Paul E. Clark, pp. 44, 54, 60, © Brian Carr, p. 47, © Bill Bachmann, p. 49; James E. Sirvaitis, pp. 14, 46 (right), 69; Ned Skubic, p. 16 (right); Root Resources: © Gail Nachel, p. 17 (right), © D. I. MacDonald, pp. 51, 59; Florida State Archives, pp. 18-19, 21, 22, 24, 28, 32, 33, 34, 35, 36, 37, 38, 62 (top right), 65 (center left, bottom); Library of Congress, p. 25; Independent Picture Service, pp. 27, 62 (top left); Neg. No. 327045, Dept. of Library Services, American Museum of Natural History, p. 29; NASA, p. 39; Jerry Hennen, p. 45; U.S. Air Force Photo by Joe Piccorossi, p. 50; Bill Simpson, Florida Department of Agriculture and Consumer Services, p. 52 (top); Olive Glasgow, p. 52 (bottom); Sylvia Schlender, pp. 52-53; Alex Kerstitch, p. 57; © Franklin & Kathy Viola, pp. 58, 61; Hollywood Book & Poster Co., pp. 62 (center left, center right, bottom), 64 (center left, center right); Rick A. Kolodziej, p. 63 (top left); © Carol Newsom, p. 63 (top right); Houston Astros, p. 63 (bottom left); Rosica, Mulhern & Assoc., p. 63 (bottom right); Special Collections, University of South Florida Library, p. 64 (top left); Merrill Lynch & Co., Inc., p. 64 (top right); MCA Records, p. 64 (bottom); Department of Justice, p. 65 (top left); Cuban Archival Collection, Otto G. Richter Library, Univ. of Miami, Coral Gables, FL, p. 65 (top right); Fisk Archives, Fisk University, p. 65 (center right); Jean Matheny, p. 66; Wm. J. Tacheny, p. 70.